Seen Grandpa Lately?

Other books for children by Roy Fuller
Stories
Savage Gold
Catspaw

Poetry
Poor Roy

ROY FULLER

Seen Grandpa Lately?

Illustrated by Joan Hickson

 ANDRE DEUTSCH

First published 1972 by
André Deutsch Limited
105 Great Russell Street London WC1
Second Impression 1979

Copyright © 1972 by Roy Fuller
All rights reserved

Printed in Great Britain by
The Anchor Press Ltd and bound by
Wm Brendon & Son Ltd both of
Tiptree, Essex

ISBN 0 233 96118 6

s, all nouns and verbs; five years
fore these win her ears.
ing of a table is

ile upon her phiz.
to inflame or bore:
e works of Scott, she tore
odstock. Such a critic makes
n time judge mine as fakes.

'TV' was written for a record issued by Jupiter Recordings. I am grateful to them for prompting me to write it – and even more to Ann Thwaite, editor of *Allsorts* (in which several of these poems have been printed), who later fanned the interest I had in writing poems that children might like. I should also mention the kind approach of Kaye Webb, editor of *Puffin News*, where 'A Boy's Clothes' first appeared. Other poems have been previously published in *The Listener* and *Child Education*.

R.F.

Contents

Bringing up babies 9
The National Union of Children 10
The National Association of Parents 11
Girl making pies 12
TV 13
Teresa nude 15
Cherry time 17
Drawing 18
A boy's clothes 20
A boy's friend 21
Child wondering 22
Ermyntrude 23
Horrible things 24
The start of a memorable holiday 25
In the restaurant 27
Australia 29
Epitaphs 31
Stables' tables 33
Advice to poets 36
The poet 37
The poets 38
The minstrel 41
After the poetry-reading 42
Names 43

To my grand-daughter, learning the flute   44
Bees in August   44
Autumn   45
After breakfast   45
The retired man goes shopping   46
The 4 a.m. bluebottle   47
Song   48
Starlings   49
Snow   49
Nature   50
At the garden bowl again   51
The world through the window   52
Take-over by the garden   53
The dream   54
A memory of Kenya   55
Bicycle handlebars   55
Advice to children   56
Happy lion   58
The Courts   59
An English explorer   60
The art of the possible   61
Tails on fairy tales   62

Bringing up babies

If babies could speak they'd tell mother or nurse
That slapping was pointless, and why:
For if you're not crying it prompts you to cry,
And if you are – then you cry worse.

The National Union of Children

NUC has just passed a weighty resolution:
'Unless all parents raise our rate of pay
This action will be taken by our members
(The resolution comes in force today): –

'Noses will not be blown (sniffs are in order),
Bedtime will get preposterously late,
Ice-cream and crisps will be consumed for breakfast,
Unwanted cabbage left upon the plate,

'Earholes and finger-nails can't be inspected,
Overtime (known as homework) won't be worked,
Reports from school will all say "Could do better",
Putting bricks back in boxes may be shirked.'

The National Association of Parents

Of course, NAP's answer quickly was forthcoming
(It was a matter of emergency),
It issued to the Press the following statement
(Its Secretary appeared upon TV): –

'True that the so-called Saturday allowance
Hasn't kept pace with prices in the shops,
But neither have, alas, parental wages:
NUC's claim would ruin kind, hard-working Pops.

'Therefore, unless that claim is now abandoned,
Strike action for us, too, is what remains;
In planning for the which we are in process
Of issuing, to all our members, canes.'

Girl making pies

When my mother's making pies
I usually make one, too.
Mine is always midget size
And it never seems to rise.

Mother's pies are very tasty
And yet whatever I do
Mine are almost only pastry:
You could nearly call them nasty.

Into hers you couldn't cram
More stuff or else they'd burst:
In mine there's just a hint of lamb,
One currant or a vein of jam.

But Dad must like them best, because
He eats the grey things first;
For once not saying, as he gnaws:
'Go and wash those filthy paws.'

TV

In the coloured world of home
there's a greyish oblong hole;
and it's the only thing that
moves among the furniture.

Somewhere past the couch tiny
clouds and horses spring into
view and disappear before
they get to the window-sill.

Though these things and beings are
so small, their noise is human.
Passing empty rooms, you hear
gun-shots and angry talking.

Even when there is no one
to see or hear it, this life
in the curved glass probably
goes on just the same. Who knows?

Our universe began in
a concentrated atom.
So does this screen of shadows
when you first switch on the knob.

It also ends like that as
you switch the other way, though
first the sound dies, and all yell,
but cannot make themselves heard.

POSTSCRIPT: ON THE ARRIVAL OF COLOUR

In the greyish world of home
there's a coloured oblong hole;
and naturally we all sit
with our red eyes glued on it.

Teresa nude

Teresa bathing, glancing down, said: 'Mummy,
I wonder what it looks like in my tummy.'

The answer: pictures in a range of inks
From deepest scarlet to indifferent pinks.

– Though possibly the liver, some would deem,
Being purplish-brown, outside this colour-scheme.

And pale the bowels' wrinkled furbelows,
Packaged as neatly as a brand-new hose.

Though in the 'tummy' scarcely to be placed,
The fiery lung-trees grow up from the waist.

And a few miscellaneous parts propel
Juices and dinners through the hues of hell.

Teresa, thanks for acting as our guide
To all the beauteous sights we have inside.

Yet better we should merely show our skin,
Be made not inside out but inside in –

For how could we be ever calmly viewed
If the above were what we looked like nude?

Cherry time

Where Chloë has been sitting lie
Scatterings of humeri
From petite and green-boned peoples;
And as many shrunken skulls.
I wonder she could bear to sit
So long in that burial pit.

Drawing

Small boys and girls can draw a house
But find it hard to draw a mouse.

Most drawing in a house is square:
Square walls and windows in square air.

– Though from the chimneys, I don't doubt,
Nothing square can ever come out.

But smoke is really only scribble:
Not so the beast that loves to nibble.

You'd need a film to show a nose
That always quivers as it goes.

Even invisible ink wouldn't meet
The problem of tiny rapid feet.

If you were colouring the fur –
Grey or brown, which would you prefer?

And were you getting down the tail
And put a corner in, you'd fail.

And how to show those long front teeth,
The bottom lip tucked underneath;

The upper ditto very bristly?
Your style would have to be quite Whistlery.

Besides, a mouse would never keep still
Long enough to let you draw it well.

And were one brought in by the cat
You'd be too sad to copy that.

Strange that a mixture of curves and hair
Likes living in a thing so square:

It could, were it self-advertising,
Make life and art much more surprising.

A boy's clothes

In bed I see my clothes
Over the chair and floor,
And wonder at the shape
That they were tailored for.

Bent on a wizened chest,
Two handless arms repose;
The legs are short and wide,
The severed feet lack toes.

Though when I go downstairs
No one cries out in fright:
Apparently I manage
To make the things look right.

But thickness must seem strange
To that creature by the bed;
My movements ghostly and
Superfluous my head.

A boy's friend

I have a secret friend
With whom I never quarrel.
I'm Watson to his Holmes,
He's Hardy to my Laurel.

I'm greedy for his calls
And leave him with sad heart.
He thinks of marvellous games.
He mends what comes apart.

Though when he isn't here
I can't recall his face,
I'm always glancing at
That slightly freckled space.

His name's quite ordinary
But seems unusual.
His brain's stocked like a shop.
His talk is comical.

Often with other friends
Play ends in biffs and screams:
With him, play calmly goes
Through dusk – and even dreams.

Child wondering

I wonder what I used to be
Before I started out as me.
I remember crawling on the floor
But hardly anything before.
Yet sometimes waking in the dark
I see a little turning spark
As though another world had once
Impressed itself upon my glance;
And hear a train I never hear
In daytime anywhere so near;
And think that in the whole of space
To be in bed's the oddest place,
Forgetting quite how safe it seemed
Before I fell asleep and dreamed.

When morning comes and sunlight falls
On maps and faces on the walls,
And birds are saying what can be
Hummed but not understood by me;
And reading in my bedside books
Of pies made out of singing rooks,
And the complaints by nervous bears
Of girls whose bottoms dint their chairs –
Gradually I start to feel
The realness of the strangely real;
And by the time I cut my bacon
Know that I'm probably mistaken
To think it's any use to wonder
What lies behind, in front, out yonder.

Ermyntrude

A little girl named Ermyntrude
Was often curiously rude –
Came down to breakfast in the nude.
Her sister said (though not a prude):
'It seems to me extremely crude
To see your tummy over food:
Your conduct borders on the lewd.

Also, you nastily exude
Cornflakes and milk as though you'd spewed' –
Her lips were open when she chewed,
And read a comic-book called *Dude*.
She was a sight not to be viewed
Without profound disquietude.
Though what could come but such a mood
From anyone named Ermyntrude?

Horrible things

'What's the horriblest thing you've seen?'
Said Nell to Jean.

'Some grey-coloured, trodden-on plasticine;
On a plate, a left-over cold baked bean;
A cloak-room ticket numbered thirteen;
A slice of meat without any lean;
The smile of a spiteful fairy-tale queen;
A thing in the sea like a brown submarine;
A cheese fur-coated in brilliant green;
A bluebottle perched on a piece of sardine.
What's the horriblest thing *you've* seen?'
Said Jean to Nell.

'Your face, as you tell
Of all the horriblest things you've seen.'

The start of a memorable holiday

Good evening, sir. Good evening, ma'am. Good evening,
   little ladies.
From all the staff, a hearty welcome to the Hotel Hades.
Oh yes, sir, since you booked your rooms we have been
   taken over
And changed our name – but for the better – as you'll soon
   discover.
Porter, Room 99! Don't worry, sir – just now he took
Much bulkier things than bags on his pathetic iron hook.
The other room, the children's room? I'm very pleased to say
We've put them in the annexe, half a mile across the way.
They'll have a nearer view there of the bats' intriguing
   flying,
And you, dear sir and madam, won't be troubled by their
   crying
– Although I'm sure that neither of them's frightened of the
   gloom.
Besides, the maid will try to find a candle for their room.

Of course, ma'am, we've a maid there, she's the porter's (seventh) wife:
She'll care for these dear children quite as well as her own life.
The journey's tired them? Ah, tonight they won't be counting sheep!
I'll see they have a nice hot drink before they're put to sleep.
Don't be too late yourselves, sir, for the hotel's evening meal:
I hope that on the menu will be some roast milk-fed veal.
If you'll forgive me, I must stoke the ovens right away:
It's going to be (excuse the joke) hell in this place today!
Yes, I do all the cooking *and* the getting of the meat:
Though we're so far from shops we've usually something fresh to eat.
Of course, it isn't always veal, and when the school terms start
Joints may get tougher. But our gravy still stays full of heart!

In the restaurant

Said the waiter to the bald man:
'Have you studied the bill of fare?'
Said the bald man to the waiter:
'I'd like a portion of hare.'

His wife said: 'Were you choosing,
What would you choose?' said she.
'Not corn on the cob,' said the waiter.
'My own corn's killing me.'

Their guest, puzzling over the menu,
Said: 'I'll have the Angus Game.'
'I'm sorry, sir,' said the waiter,
'That's the proprietor's name.'

Said a man at the next table
In a voice like a bell's deep toll
(He was wearing a clerical collar):
'Don't overlook the sole.'

'I'm very fond of Stilton,
Cheddar and Brie, so please,'
Said a little chap in the corner,
'I'd like some of your lychees.'

A table for six in the middle
Had to seat a crowd of fourteen.
Said they, when they ordered their starters:
'We all rather feel like sardines.'

A Red Indian came through the doorway
(His squaw shouldered their papoose).
'I've been hunting all day,' he shouted,
'And I want an extra large mousse.'

– Followed by an actor, saying
In tones deliberately droll
(He was 'resting' at the moment):
'And *I* want a nice big roll.'

Said the proprietor to the waiter:
'These customers make me ill.
Give them all duck or turkey,
And don't forget the bill.'

Australia

Quite obviously in Australia
Everything's upside down;
And you must be an absolute failure
If you happen to wear a crown.

Do you walk, to get through a door,
On the ceiling? Does a bird
Perch out of harm on the floor?
Is 'top' a rather rude word?

Is headball played, and elevennis?
If you hate anyone is it love?
Of course, they don't know where heaven is
Except that it's not up above.

Are holidays longer than terms?
Are humbugs good for you?
No doubt deep in the sky are worms,
And served first is the last in the queue.

Do dogs sniff each others' noses
And wag them when they are glad?
Are dandelions not roses
Carefully grown by Dad?

Do children go to the office?
Does Mother tell awful lies?
And Grandpa buy comics and toffees,
Gran's skirt give her chilly thighs?

If so, I'll not go to Australia,
Where at jokes a listener sobs.
Besides, I prefer a dahlia
To grow flowers rather than knobs.

Epitaphs

Here lies a careless boy named Gunn
Who fed a lion with a bun.
At least, in one hand held a bun
But, typically, fed the other one.

*

A man called Percy Brown lies here
Who used to sip his father's beer.
And later on he sipped his own:
His weight at death was forty stone.

*

Here lies a greedy girl, Jane Bevan,
Whose breakfasts hardly ever stopped.
One morning at half past eleven
She snapped and crackled and then popped.

*

A schoolmistress called Binks lies here.
She held her own for twenty year.
She pleaded, biffed, said: 'I'm your friend.'
But children got her in the end.

*

Here lies Prue Jones, whose childish folly
Was to eat too much of a lime iced lolly
And get a splinter in a place
Where splinters make a hopeless case.

Here lies John Smith, exactly eight,
Who was given a handsome chemistry set.
Here also lies his sister, Maria.
Or what was left of them after the fire.

*

Here lies Amanda Mary Wilde
Who was in fact a lying child.
Her end came as she told a whopper
While sucking a halfpenny gob-stopper.

*

Here lies a family dog called Rover:
His pampered life at last is over.
On Rover more than on each other
Love was bestowed by Dad and Mother.

*

Here lies a precocious, insomniac tot
Who knew how to let down the side of his cot.
He undid the catches one evening at seven
And, the bars having vanished, fell straight up to heaven.

Stables' tables

There was a girl called Sheila Stables
Who never really knew her tables.
At least, with study she was able
To get to know the twice times table;
Then having had revealed the trick,
She learned her ten times fairly quick.
A friend of hers called Mabel Gimpel
Said five and eleven were just as simple,
But Sheila never found this so.
Particularly hard to know
Were nine and seven times. Miss Bass
(Who took the mathematics class)
Would call out: 'Sheila Stables, what
Are seven nines? . . . Oh no, they're not.'

Her bad marks in this subject rather
Worried her. She told her father,
Who laughed and said: 'Why goodness me,
There are more vital matters, She,
Than learning boring things by heart –
For instance, human love, and art.'
A poetic man was Mr Stables
Who'd never quite got right *his* tables
And if required to do a sum
Would use four fingers and a thumb.

'What's nine times seven?' asked Miss Bass.
'Only, my father says, an ass
Would know the answer,' Sheila said,

Though not without a sense of dread.
'I asked you, not your father,' Miss
Bass cried. 'Nought out of ten for this.'

Whether in later life She Stables
Had ever mastered all her tables
I do not know, but she became
A greater player of the game
Than even the formidable Bass.
She worked out when the sun would pass
Behind the planet Minotaur
(A body quite unknown before
The book of astronomic tables
Compiled by Dr Sheila Stables);
And put, the right way up, a bit
Of puzzle Einstein failed to fit.

It seemed the world did not depend
On having at one's fingers' end
Nine eights or seven sixes – though
Poetry itself could never show
(As Sheila was the first to say)
The Past, the Purpose and the Way:
Somewhere among the curious laws
Enacted by the Primal Cause
There enters (usually in the heavens)
Such things as nine, or seven, sevens.

Advice to poets

If you lack an inventive brain
Writing a poem is hell.
Choose a form that has a refrain,

Then the subsequent stanzas' strain
You'll be able to bear fairly well.
If you lack an inventive brain

Before (as I'm trying to explain)
Even starting your doggerel
Choose a form that has a refrain.

Forms help to keep poets sane
(A good one's the villanelle
If you lack an inventive brain),

For most poets compose with pain
And this tip will some pain dispel –
Choose a form that has a refrain.

Get one line or, preferably, twain;
Go on ringing them like a bell:
If you lack an inventive brain
Choose a form. That has a refrain.

The poet

The heron is more than a hero,
While the starling is only a stare:
And though one is bigger than zero
It looks rather lean when it's bare.

Why do I write down such stanzas?
It's not that I'm cracked or jocose,
But some think such extravaganzas
Guarantee that they're not reading prose.

The poets

Though Shakespeare's our national bard
His poetry's terribly hard.
It would benefit those
Who were sitting their 'O's
If in *Lear* it was Noddy who starred.

★

In the muscular verse of John Donne
There's not a great deal of clean fun;
So until you're on terms
With women or worms
He's one of the poets to shun.

★

Would he ever have stayed at the Hilton,
That Puritan poet called Milton?
Of course the polemic
Is quite academic –
In *his* day Park Lane wasn't built on.

★

In the era of Dryden and Pope
Poets didn't write adverts for soap.
They earned their reward
By soft-soaping some lord,
And washed with cold water and hope.

★

What else may be said against Blake
He certainly wasn't a fake.
Some poems were mad,
Many more very bad,
But a few make the reader's voice shake.

★

The Scot loves the poems of Burns
Save some he high-mindedly spurns:
Though oddly enough
That rather rude stuff
Is just what the Englishman learns.

★

To find if a man is scoundrelly
Ask: 'Do you like Keats more than Shelley?'
This test you can do
On but one or two,
Since these poets aren't featured on telly.

★

A poem addressed to Lord Tennyson
Has got to avoid the rhyme 'venison'
Which sounds quite obscene
Close to one whom the Queen
Endowed with her personal benison.

★

Some people say 'W. B. Yeats'
To rhyme with another bard, Keats.
The fault is not great
Since mere mention of Yeats
Puts a speaker among the aesthetes.

The minstrel

I came into the hall
Out of the biting squall:
The snow lay on my shoulders like a shawl.

I heard the monarch call,
Raising his goblet tall,
For a tale to hold the company in thrall –

That told of some great fall
And nicely would appall
Those safely sheltered from the weather's brawl.

I saw fissures in the wall
And things that freely crawl
Over the stones of Egypt, Carthage, Gaul;

And then began to bawl
The tale told by us all,
That starts thuswise: 'I came into the hall . . .'

After the poetry-reading

In the bar of the National Book League
When the poetry-reading was done,
The poets and their admirers
Met for coffee and a bun.

A few had bought books of poems
Which the poets were asked to sign:
Thinking of each one and sixpence,
They signed on the dotted line.

Talking to elderly ladies,
Their eyes on the girls in the throng,
They wondered if this were the purpose
Of growing their hair so long.

Names

Before I was christened my grandfather said
That what they proposed to call me – Roy –
Was the name of a big black dog, not a boy;
And he knew about names because his was Fred.

Suppose you could choose, what name would you pick?
Almost certainly never the name you've got.
But the trouble is, that though you think you're not,
You really are Cyril or Sydney or Dick.

And only in tales is the hero called
Peregrine, Lancelot or Captain Blood:
The man who does deeds of actual good
Is usually something like Archibald.

And so the lesson seems perfectly plain:
You can make a name, not the name make you.
And big black dogs need not form the view
That I took their name entirely in vain.

To my grand-daughter, learning the flute

Many can play on the flute
With lips that are fat or hirsute.
So those who possess perfect bows
Will flute them to shame, I suppose.
And since elegant Handel sonatas
Emerge through moustached split tomatoes,
From cherries there may well be blown
Forms of beauty so far unknown.
The gadget itself, come to think,
Started out as the virtuous Syrinx.

Bees in August

It's rather unfair they should not only smell
But gobble the lavender blossom as well.

Autumn

Sweeping up leaves, I come
across a few dead blooms
I just don't remember
growing in summer – queer
pink-striped stalks; and some
purple cone shapes – mushrooms?
'Last week's Fifth November,'
I think, and all is clear.

After breakfast

I stop myself sliding a morsel
Of bacon fat into the bin.
It will do as a meal for the robin,
His legs are so terribly thin.

The retired man goes shopping

In the middle of the morning I often go out,
Passing pensioners pushing their baskets on wheels,
And babies in strollers by mothers in rollers
Who seem far too young for the job, one feels.
I'm seen as a pensioner, too, without doubt,
But I'm not yet so ancient or daft to be willing
To purchase such things as 'battered fish fingers'
Or (as the butcher prints) 'LEAN BREASTS 1/–'.

The 4 a.m. bluebottle

The fly was peacefully sleeping,
No doubt, till I turned on the light.
Now it alternates between creeping
On my nose and lunatic flight.

Shall I switch back to the gloaming
That makes insomnia worse,
Or try to put up with this roaming
That distracts me from writing verse?

I must admit I mull over
A squirt of insecticide,
But whether for me or the rover
I can't really quite decide.

Song

I like to think the thrushes sing to me:
I copy phrases of the song they know.
If they're not very far up in the tree,
Sometimes I see them cock their heads – as though

They recognised my all too human art;
As though my being near them changed the song;
As though their lives were influenced in part
By what I may have uttered in their tongue.

But even through my absence in the house
The song goes on; and then, to catch the falling
Sun, the bird climbs to higher and higher boughs,
Until the trembling throat's invisibly calling.

– Like poets singing; and how everyone
Feels he makes contact with those moving on.

Starlings

The starlings at the garden bowl
Remind me of children round a pool.
They don't allow each other in;
They hesitate upon the brink;
They all keep up a squawking din;
They make the water feculent.

However, children do not drink
Bathwater save by accident.

Snow

Snow falling in November
May fall on a yellow rose,
Forming an ice-cream cornet
That with ice-cream overflows.

When snow falls in December
It has only a bare black twig
To chalk on a sky of yellow
And make unusually big.

If snow should fall in April
How hard to tell its crumb
From petals cast in the border
Or blossom on the plum.

Nature

In their nest the birds arrange
Abstract shapes of four or five.
Do they find it very strange
Soon to see there something live?

Azure ovals, speckled brown,
Changed to bits of naked skin –
Then, relief when mouth of clown
Turns to beak's sardonic grin?

No, strangeness nor relief is there:
Nature accepts what nature works.
It's only we who seek and bear
Meanings where no meaning lurks.

At the garden bowl again

Sparrows aren't very great bathers
Though they like a dip in the dust,
But starlings queue up for the water –
Then seem able only to just
Take off with a water-logged thrust.

Pigeons can siphon the liquid
Without ever raising their beaks;
Other birds appear to be gargling
As they scoop up a billful that leaks.
But pigeons are usually freaks.

So I sit with my whisky and soda,
Observing these species of fowl,
And they in their turn watch me closely
To see if I throw back my jowl
Or suck from my own garden bowl.

The world through the window

Sometimes birds fly against the glass
Towards the boughs reflected there,
Thinking they are about to pass
Into a forest, strange and rare.

Fruits darkly glisten on each tree,
Unpierced by any other bill.
The vision stuns: occasionally,
Is even liable to kill.

It's like what we ourselves may see
The other side of that same glass –
A fire; a favourite face, settee;
Set out against the evening grass.

Below the sill our eyes alight
Upon the bird that visualised
Another world. Its eyes are tight;
Its beak is open, dumb, surprised.

Take-over by the garden

In the end, the garden creatures became more friendly.
The ladybird led by refusing to fly from our finger –
More than usually – fluffing her wings out from their cases
Then putting them very neatly back again.

The blackbird didn't stop at the threshold, but showed
The bald rings round his eyes, his earth-crumbed bill,
His white chinks in his glossy armour of black,
Among the curving chair-legs and our slippers.

And the dusty bristles of the hedgehog made
Our sofas difficult to lie on: bees
Drank with us at our bedside tumblers of water:
In the bath, living frogs as well as plastic dolphins.

And no one seemed to quarrel in front of the owl,
Standing at the end of the shelf like a loudspeaker.
Our lives were full of little important cares;
And happily this happened all the world over.

The dream

There was a dream that kept recurring:
It seemed absurd to dream that dream
In such a place, at such sad time.

Who would have known of the recurring
But for the broken stones that lean
Where parliaments of men have been? –

That in a way were like the dream,
Though falling short of its great scheme;
That were more like the dream's recurring.

A memory of Kenya

The neck of an ostrich makes a J;
And though its knee-joints bend the wrong way
It travels at almost the speed of sound,
Its head and body parallel to the ground;
And its droppings are silver waterfalls
On the hot dry plains of Africa.

Bicycle handlebars

Their shape when I was still at school
Was cows' horns, as a general rule –

Though boys whose speech was full of 'damns'
Crouched over things like horns of rams.

But now the young ride straight to hell
Bolt upright, wrestling a gazelle.

What next? Go wheeling through the dusk
Steering two tortuous mammoth's tusks?

Or at perdition's very door
Gain bovine gravity once more?

Advice to children

I
Caterpillars living on lettuce
Are the colour of their host:
Look out, when you're eating a salad,
For the greens that move the most.

Close your mouth tight when you're running
As when washing you shut your eyes,
Then as soap is kept from smarting
So will tonsils be from flies.

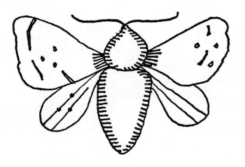

If in spite of such precautions
Anything nasty gets within,
Remember it will be thinking:
'Far worse for me than him.'

2

If in the middle of the night
Your bedside water tastes of cloth,
It means that possibly you might
By accident have drunk a moth.

In summer it's as well you should
Switch on the light before you sip,
For others actually could
Be taking then their midnight dip.

3

Plate-glass doors form a dangerous duo:
Never, when using them, try
To enter the place by the one marked TUO
Or withdraw through the one marked ИI.

4

The world is dark with rumours
And things may happen to you.
Keep your handkerchief in your bloomers
And your money in your shoe.

Happy lion

When you are really old
A mysterious lion will keep
Appearing in your dreams –
Its hide a dirty gold,
Its mane a matted heap,
Its eyes like coffee creams.

Those future dreams will prove
Deep down you've not forgotten –
That still you take to bed –
The beast you now so love:
Though then worn out its cotton,
Its stuffing long since bled.

The Courts

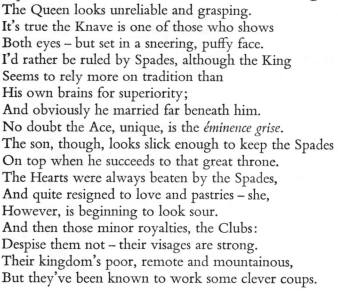

I always think the Diamond dynasty
A trifle sinister. The King displays
Only one eye: perhaps the other's patched.
The Queen looks unreliable and grasping.
It's true the Knave is one of those who shows
Both eyes – but set in a sneering, puffy face.
I'd rather be ruled by Spades, although the King
Seems to rely more on tradition than
His own brains for superiority;
And obviously he married far beneath him.
No doubt the Ace, unique, is the *éminence grise*.
The son, though, looks slick enough to keep the Spades
On top when he succeeds to that great throne.
The Hearts were always beaten by the Spades,
And quite resigned to love and pastries – she,
However, is beginning to look sour.
And then those minor royalties, the Clubs:
Despise them not – their visages are strong.
Their kingdom's poor, remote and mountainous,
But they've been known to work some clever coups.

One thing they share, these flowered families –
Dread of the proletarian Joker, who,
Though warning of his presence by his pallor,
Is always liable to take them by surprise.

An English explorer

An oblong trodden yellow packet on the pavement
Is not too dirty for its legend to be read,
Which is, mysteriously, 'Barratt's Sherbet Fountain'.
At once my thoughts to far exotic lands are led.

I see deep in the burning desert an oasis,
And there, the sudden emerald of palms among –
Perhaps a slender dancing girl or two beside it –
The sherbet fountain bubbles sherbet all day long.

And who enjoys its free and effervescent coolness
(Also enjoys the slender dancers, I suppose)?
Why, he who bravely found and named it – Mr Barratt –
Stretched by it, wearing khaki shorts and woollen hose.

The art of the possible

Ask for bunnies' ears – Notice on ice-cream van

Don't ask for automatic gears
Or Worthington's or Bass's beers
Or Scarborough or Brighton piers
Or three or even fewer cheers.

Don't ask for bandits' bandoliers
Or caliphs and their fat viziers;
Gazebos, ha-has, belvederes,
Or rapids, waterfalls and weirs.

Don't ask for eminent careers
Or universal panaceas.
Don't ask for alligators' tears
But, as you're told, for bunnies' ears.

Tails on fairy tales

What would the bears have done
To Goldilocks had they caught her?
Eaten her like a bun,
Or treated her like a daughter?

Someone to polish off the stodgy
Porridge, to warm the chairs,
In bed to put one's podgy
Arms round. Please come back upstairs!

*

For wolf as well as Grandma, a dreadful end.
Is there really between animals and humans
such an enmity?

Isn't it suspicious that to Red Riding Hood
the wolf spoke human language so fluently,
meeting in the wood?

It seems to me that had he been a real wolf
he'd have gone miles out of his way to avoid
a girl wearing red.

Who was he then, this villain in a wolf skin,
with such a smooth patter and an appetite?
Seen Grandpa lately?

*

When Jack chopped down the stalk
The giant was only stunned.
He lay there, white as chalk.

Jack's Ma came out, cried: 'Oh,
Here's your father back, who left me
Fifteen years ago.'

And soon he was eating pie
As heartily as in
His hide-out in the sky.

*

'Dear Cinderella,'
said the Prince one day,
'how would you like to
put on your old dress,
sit in the ashes?

'My subjects envy
our home and riches,
but now I've got you
such things don't matter:
I could give them up.'

'They matter to me,'
said Cinderella.
'You were never poor.
You never swept floors.
You could dance all night.'

'But, Cinderella,
look, the mob's raging
at the palace gates!'
'Then just arrest its
two ugly leaders.'

★

'Whoever heard of a cat
As Mayor of London? Who
Could possibly vote for you?
Besides, *I'm* a candidate.'

'Who killed all the mice and rats,
Working a twelve-hour day?
And who idles his time away?
I'm afraid, Sir Richard, there
Is a great change in the air.
Long live the working-cats!'